Lake
Hiking Guide

Brian Patton and Bart Robinson

Lake Louise Hiking Guide

Published by
Summerthought

Summerthought Publishing
PO Box 2309
Banff, AB T1L 1C1
Canada
www.summerthought.com

All photos © Andrew Hempstead unless otherwise noted
Design and production: Linda Petras
Printed in Canada by Friesens
Source maps from Natural Resources Canada
(http://open.canada.ca/en/open-government-licence-canada)

We gratefully acknowledge the financial support of the
Alberta Foundation for the Arts for our publishing activities.

Library and Archives Canada Cataloguing in Publication

Patton, Brian, 1943-, author
        Lake Louise hiking guide / Brian Patton and Bart Robinson.

Includes index.
ISBN 978-1-926983-33-2 (softcover)

1. Hiking--Alberta--Louise, Lake, Region--Guidebooks.   2. Trails--Alberta--
Louise, Lake, Region--Guidebooks.   3. Louise, Lake, Region (Alta.)--Guidebooks.
I. Robinson, Bart, author   II. Title.

GV199.44.C22L345 2018   796.51097123'32   C2018-900327-8

Table of Contents

Preface

When we set out to write a trail guide in 1970, the hiking trails of Banff National Park were the ones we knew best and the focus for our project. We'd hiked enough at that point in our young lives to know that this park contained more great short hikes and day trips than any similar area in North America.

While our initial plan to publish a trail guide to Banff National Park was soon replaced by the more grandiose *Canadian Rockies Trail Guide*, we knew the section on Banff—and Lake Louise in particular—would be the most-used section of the book. In addition to being Canada's most-visited national park, it contains a concentration of 18 trails in and around the Lake Louise region, all of which can be completed in a day or less. Many of these trips include high alpine lakes along the way or as a primary destination—a big plus for most hikers. Other trails lead to high viewpoints overlooking the Bow Valley and glaciated peaks.

So, many years after originally planning a guidebook dedicated to Banff, we have created the *Lake Louise Hiking Guide*. This book contains more elements of value to the walker and day-hiker than the *Canadian Rockies Trail Guide*, including useful and interesting facts about each trail, colour topographical maps, and colour photographs. Most importantly, for us personally, this book is an opportunity to highlight the trails that have been a special part of our lives for over four decades. There isn't a single trail in this book that we haven't hiked on numerous occasions and at all the months of the hiking season. We hope you receive as much pleasure from these trips as we have.

About the Authors

For over 40 years, Brian Patton has interpreted the natural and human history of the Canadian Rockies, including stints with CBC Radio, The Banff Centre, the Whyte Museum of the Canadian Rockies, and as a naturalist working for Parks Canada. He has also appeared as an historical interpreter and storyteller in five documentary films about the region. He is also the author of the *Canadian Rockies Trail Guide*, *Parkways of the Canadian Rockies*, *Tales from the Canadian Rockies*, *Mountain Chronicles: Jon Whyte* and *Bear Tales from the Canadian Rockies*. He continues to work on a variety projects from his home in Invermere, British Columbia.

Following the publication of the original *Canadian Rockies Trail Guide*, Bart Robinson authored several books on the Canadian Rockies: *Banff Springs: The Story of a Hotel, Columbia Icefield: A Solitude of Ice* and *Great Days in the Rockies: The Photographs of Byron Harmon*. Subsequently, he has enjoyed a long career as a journalist, editor, and conservationist. He was an editor with Equinox magazine from 1982 to 1994, and the Executive Director of the Yellowstone to Yukon Conservation Initiative from 1996 to 2003. He currently lives in Canmore, Alberta.

Lower Consolation Lake

There are few hiking areas in the world that can rival Lake Louise for the accessibility of stunning mountain scenery. In the Lake Louise region are 18 designated hikes and over 76 kilometres (47 miles) of trail traversing some of the most rugged alpine scenery on the continent.

Introduction

Hiking History at Lake Louise

Lake Louise is the birthplace of recreational hiking in the Canadian Rockies. Soon after the erection of the first rustic chalet on the lake's shoreline in 1890, manager Willoughby Astley began clearing trails to scenic points above the lake. In 1893, a pair of young adventurers from the eastern U.S., Walter Wilcox and Samuel Allen, began a systematic exploration of the region. The following summer, they returned to Lake Louise with three fellow Yale students, during which time they discovered and explored Paradise Valley, Sentinel Pass and the upper end of the Valley of the Ten Peaks, and completed the first ascent of

Walter Wilcox (far right) and his Yale classmates spent the summer of 1894 exploring the Lake Louise region and named many lakes and peaks.
Credit: Whyte Museum of the Canadian Rockies (na66-2251)

Mount Temple (3,544 metres/11,630 feet), which was the first ascent of a Canadian peak above 11,000 feet. In 1899, Wilcox and a companion made the first recorded visit to Moraine Lake and nearby Consolation Valley. Wilcox and Allen named many local features, and their explorations led to further trail construction by the Canadian Pacific Railway (CPR). As these trails became popular, the CPR built tea houses and shelters at strategic locations. In fact, hotel staff maintained much of the local trail system through the mid-20th century.

Indigenous people called Lake Louise "Lake of Little Fishes" and if you look carefully while walking the Lakeshore trail you may see why.

Lake Agnes Tea House in the early 1900s.
Credit: Whyte Museum of the Canadian Rockies (v465-pd2-237)

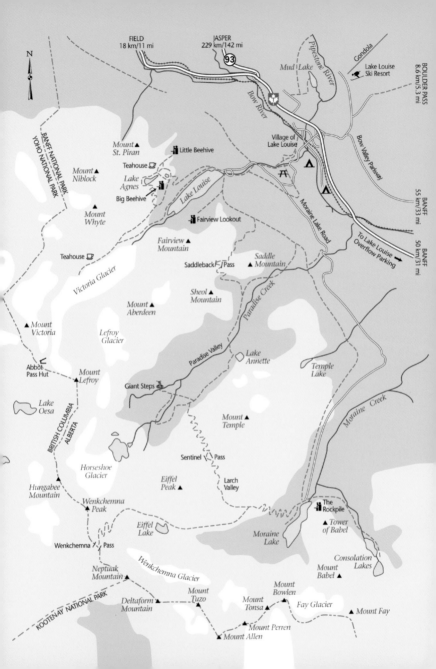

Using This Book

THE REGIONS

The trails in the *Lake Louise Hiking Guide* are organized by the following regions:

Village of Lake Louise: The village of Lake Louise lies on the valley floor, a 40-minute drive northwest of the town of Banff and a two-hour drive west of Calgary.

Lake Louise: The lake itself is an eight-minute drive from the village along Lake Louise Drive. All trails at Lake Louise start from the lakeshore.

Paradise Valley: Located between Lake Louise and Moraine Lake, only one trail leads up this valley, but it's a highlight for serious hikers.

Moraine Lake: Accessed by road from Lake Louise Drive, Moraine Lake is the starting point for hikes leading into sublime alpine scenery.

Whitehorn-Slate Range: Across the valley from Lake Louise, a gondola takes the hard work out of reaching the alpine zone, or head off to Boulder Pass, gateway to the famous Skoki Valley.

NEED TO KNOW

The introductory information for each trail will help you decide if it is appropriate for your ability and how much time you have. It includes the following elements:

Length: Whenever a trail runs out and back on the same route, distances quoted are one-way. But for loop trips (circuits), total distance is provided.

Elevation gain: This is the total ascent, in metres (and feet), over the one-way course of the trail.

Walking time: The length of time it will take to reach your objective. In the case of loop trips, total time is presented. Anyone of moderate fitness can complete the trails in the time allotted. Strong hikers will need less time, but if you stop for lunch or frequent breaks it will take you a little longer.

Rating: The hiking trails in this book vary greatly in length and difficulty. Rather than designate a difficulty factor, we have applied the following terms: Easy walk (usually less than one hour and with minimal elevation gain); Short hike (elevation gain varies, but these trails can be completed in three hours or less); Moderate hike (usually three to four hours with considerable elevation gain); Day trip (a day trip doesn't necessarily mean you'll spend a full day hiking, but rather, at least four hours).

Season: These are the optimum months for hiking.

Moraine Lake from the Rockpile (opposite).

Weather

Despite the northerly latitude of the range, the Canadian Rockies experience climate and weather patterns that compare closely with higher mountain ranges further south. For example, temperature and annual precipitation in Lake Louise are similar to those of West Yellowstone, Montana, and Leadville, Colorado.

Lake Louise Climate averages

	May	June	July	Aug.	Sept.	Oct.
Maximum temp °C	12.8°	17.2°	20.4°	20.1°	14.3°	7.9°
Minimum temp °C	-1.7°	2.1°	3.6°	3.1°	-0.8°	-5.3°
Precipitation /mm	43.0	54.6	61.3	54.0	45.3	38.9

Spring (mid-April to late June) in Lake Louise is notable for long days of sunlight (in late June it stays light until 10 p.m.) and a sense of optimism for the upcoming warm months, although Lake Louise is often frozen well into June and snow is still present on most local hiking trails. The average daytime high in June is 17°C (62.5°F) and there is an average of 16.5 hours of daylight each day.

Summer (late June to mid-Sept.) is definitely high season for hiking, especially the school holiday period of July through August. Simply said, the weather is unbeatable. The season is dominated by long, warm–and sometimes hot–days, all trails are snow-free, and there's plenty to do and see. The average daytime high in both July and August is slightly over 20°C (68°F).

By early October, many high elevation trails are covered in snow. Pictured is Ptarmigan Lake photographed on October 3. Credit: Chuck O'Callaghan

Early fall (September to early October) can be delightful, especially September, with lingering warm temperatures and a noticeable decrease in crowds immediately after the long weekend (at the beginning of the month). While fall colours in general lack the intensity of those in the eastern provinces and New England, larch along the Little Beehive, Saddleback, Paradise Valley, Larch Valley, and Boulder Pass trails turn a brilliant yellow in the second half of September. The average daytime high in September is 14.3°C (57.7°F) while in October the average drops to 7.9°C (46.2°F).

For seven-day weather forecasts in Banff National Park call (403) 762-2088 or go online to www.weather.gc.ca.

Dangers and Annoyances

Compared to many of the world's wild regions, Banff National Park is a relatively benign area when it comes to dangerous beasts and other natural hazards. Yet there are a few creatures, both great and small, worthy of discussion.

WILDLIFE

The Lake Louise area has a healthy population of grizzly bears, although they are rarely encountered on the busiest trails. Regardless, always be prepared for an unexpected bear encounter and, even more importantly, to follow a few basic rules to avoid the encounter in the first place:

Check trail reports at the Lake Louise Visitor Centre for a listing of local trails where bears have been sighted. Warnings will also be posted at trailheads when bears are present.

Watch for bear sign, such as fresh droppings, diggings, or tracks. If you come across an animal carcass, leave the area immediately.

Always stay alert. You don't want to come upon a bear suddenly at close range. You should continually scan your surroundings, and peruse the slopes and valley ahead before descending from a pass or ridge.

Make noise in areas where bears have been seen or any prime bear habitat where visibility is limited. The occasional loud shout or whistle will alert bears to your presence. Talking loudly or singing can also be effective.

Groups of four or more hikers have far less chance of being charged or attacked. Nearly all serious attacks in the park have occurred when a single individual encountered a bear at close range.

Bear pepper spray has proven effective in driving away aggressive bruins, but for maximum safety each member of the hiking party should be carrying a can and it should be readily accessible.

It is beyond the scope of this book to get into all the variables that must be considered during an encounter with an aggressive bear or a bear attack. Parks Canada publishes excellent brochures covering all aspects of avoidance and what to do in an attack situation. Pick one up at a park visitor centre and read it thoroughly.

There are no other mammals that pose a significant threat to hikers in the Lake Louise region. While animals such as cougar and wolverine have fierce reputations, they are usually very shy around humans and very rarely seen in the area.

Of course, there are records of nearly every species having charged or chomped humans at one time or another. (These include an irate mother spruce grouse that permanently scarred one of the authors.) The golden rule around wildlife: always give animals room and never harass or feed them.

Grizzly bears are common in the Lake Louise region.

Bear warnings are posted at trailheads when a bear has been seen in the area.

TRAIL RESTRICTIONS

Whenever grizzly bears take up residence in the Moraine Lake-Paradise Valley environs, special restrictions are enacted requiring hikers to travel in a tight group of four or more. These restrictions have been commonplace since 1999, usually from late June/mid-July until closure of the Moraine Lake Road in mid-October. Restrictions when in place apply to Consolation Lakes, Larch Valley, Sentinel Pass, Eiffel Lake, Wenkchemna Pass, Sheol Valley, and Paradise Valley.

While it is usually not too difficult to connect with other hikers to form a group of four at Moraine Lake trailheads, never consider a trip into Paradise Valley unless you organize a group in advance and all members agree to the itinerary.

TICKS AND OTHER INSECTS

Wood ticks are abundant in dry, grassy areas of Banff National Park in spring (early May through late June). Although ticks in the Canadian Rockies have been free of Rocky Mountain Spotted Fever and Lyme disease (so far), they can cause a potentially fatal tick paralysis if they burrow at the base of the skull. The best precaution is to wear long pants tucked into socks or gaiters and to avoid lounging about on grassy slopes. Always check your clothing and body carefully following a spring hike. When a tick is discovered, a simple touch or gentle tug often dislodges it. If it has already burrowed into the skin, grasp it as close to the skin as possible with tweezers and pull firmly but slowly. If you can't remove it, or mouthparts remain in the skin, see a doctor.

Mosquitoes are generally less of a problem here than they are in the mountains and wetlands farther north. However, some summers are worse than others and certain areas are renowned for their bloodsucking hordes. Hikers do not need headnets or bug jackets, but repellent should be carried throughout the hiking season until early September.

Horseflies are another common nuisance during midsummer. Insect repellent has no effect on these large biting flies, and a heavy shirt and pants are your only protection.

GIARDIA

Another addition to the list of hiker miseries is giardia lamblia, a waterborne parasite that can cause severe and prolonged gastrointestinal distress. Giardia is carried by many species of animals, but the human infective strain is most frequently found in beaver. While the parasite finds its way into mountain streams and rivers through the feces of many animals, beaver are best equipped to perpetuate the parasite in wilderness water systems.

Some hikers are willing to take their chances in the upper portions of watersheds, particularly above treeline or where they feel secure there is no beaver activity or human sources of contamination. But the only way to be totally safe is to bring a water purification device or bottled water.

THEFT

Vehicle break-ins in Banff National Park are rare but do occur. Vehicles left overnight at trailheads are particularly prone. Use common sense and don't leave any valuables in your vehicle. If possible, keep all personal belongings out of sight by leaving them in the trunk. Report break-ins or suspicious behavior to the RCMP in Lake Louise (403/522-3811) or Banff (403/762-2226).

Planning Your Trip

Unless you are simply going for a short stroll along the shoreline of Lake Louise or Moraine Lake, exploring the local trail system requires some advance planning. In addition to practical information in this section, you can use this book to identify which trails suit your abilities and interests in advance of arriving.

While Lake Louise is best known for its natural beauty, the region also offers an excellent tourism infrastructure. Facilities such as accommodations, restaurants, and gas stations are concentrated in the village of Lake Louise. This allows visitors to spend the day hiking through the wilderness, and then soothe sore muscles in a European-style spa, dine at an upscale restaurant, and rest their heads at a luxurious lodge. For those looking for a simpler experience, campgrounds and a hostel are also within walking distance of the village.

In addition to accommodations and restaurants, the village of Lake Louise has the following services: gas stations, postal outlet, ATM, RCMP (police) detachment, medical clinic, grocery store, liquor store, retailers including a bookstore and another selling outdoor apparel and equipment, and public washrooms.

GETTING TO LAKE LOUISE

Lake Louise is along the Trans-Canada Highway 56 kilometres (35 miles) northwest of Banff, 180 kilometres (112 miles) west of Calgary, 230 kilometres (143 miles) south of Jasper, and 800 kilometres (500 miles) east of Vancouver.

From the Trans-Canada Highway interchange, the road to Lake Louise passes through the village of Lake Louise. Samson Mall and the Lake Louise Visitor Centre are in the village core, and two gas stations, restaurants, hotels and a hostel are nearby. Lake Louise Campground, one of the park's largest, is just over one kilometre (0.6 miles) from this busy intersection.

Lake Louise Drive climbs west from the village for 5.5 kilometres (3.4 miles) to Lake Louise, where parking is available in one of several large lots just south of the Fairmont Chateau Lake Louise, which is the starting point for most local trails.

PARKING AT LAKE LOUISE

Our advice is simple—arrive early to be assured a parking spot at Lake Louise, which has limited parking. To be assured of a spot, plan on arriving before 9am—and preferably before 8am.

When the parking lot at Lake Louise is full, visitors will be directed to the Lake Louise Overflow parking lot, eight kilometres (five miles) south of the village along the Trans-Canada Highway, where free shuttle buses are available. Shuttles to the lake depart the Lake Louise Overflow parking lot between mid-May and early October daily 8am to 4:30pm.

If you are staying in the village of Lake Louise or in the campground, it is easiest to travel through the valley on foot, with the Bow River Loop (see page 28) linking most points within the village. For daytrippers, parking in Samson Mall is limited to two hours. Full day parking is provided in a parking lot behind the Husky gas station. An alternative is to park at the Lake Louise Ski Resort and use their free shuttle to reach the village and lake. For details, visit: www.skilouise.com.

Visit the Parks Canada webpage: http://pc.gc.ca/banffnow for up-to-date traffic and parking status throughout the park.

Parks Canada has a number of helpful PDF brochures, including *Public Transit in Banff National Park*, that can be downloaded from this page: http://pc.gc.ca/en/pn-np/ab/banff/visit/brochures.

MORAINE LAKE ROAD

Moraine Lake Road begins from Lake Louise Drive, and runs for 12.5 kilometres (7.5 miles) to a parking area at Moraine Lake. Due to heavy snowfall and the risk of avalanches, Moraine Lake Road is only open between late May and the second Monday in October (Canadian Thanksgiving).

Parking at Moraine Lake is limited. The road is only open when parking spots at the lake are available. When the parking lot is full, the road closes until spaces become available. Note that there are no designated places to wait along Lake Louise Drive until the road opens and you are not permitted to wait at the traffic control point at the beginning of Moraine Lake Road. The road closure also applies to those accessing the Paradise Valley trailhead.

The best way to ensure you are able to access Moraine Lake is to arrive early in the morning—preferably before 8am.

During the last two weeks of September, which is the busiest time of year at Moraine Lake, shuttle buses operate daily from the Lake Louise

The view from Moraine Lake Road

Overflow parking area. During this period, RVs are not permitted on the Moraine Lake Road.

CAMPGROUND

Lake Louise Campground is on the valley floor within walking distance of the village via the Bow River Loop trail (see page 28). Exit the Trans-Canada Highway at the Lake Louise interchange, 56 kilometres (35 miles) northwest of Banff, and take the first left after crossing under the railway bridge to reach the entrance to the campground.

The campground is divided into two sections by the Bow River. Just under 200 serviced (powered) sites are grouped together on the east side of the Bow River. This section is for RVs and hard-sided trailers only. In addition to hookups, this section has showers and flush toilets. On the west side of the river are 206 unserviced sites, each with a fire ring and picnic table. This section of the campground is surrounded by an electric fence designed to separate campers and bears. It is for tent campers and tent trailers only. Amenities include kitchen shelters and a modern bathroom complex complete with hot showers.

Between June and September, campsites should be booked well in advance. Make reservations through the **Parks Canada Campground Reservation Service** (877/737-3783, www.reservation.pc.gc.ca) starting in mid-January. If you're traveling in July or August and know which dates you'll be in Lake Louise, it is strongly advised to take advantage of this service and book as early in January as you can.

On most nights in summer every campsite in Lake Louise will have been reserved far in advance. When the campground is full, campers are directed to an overflow area beside the Trans-Canada Highway eight kilometres (five miles) south of the village. This glorified parking lot has no designated sites, but is the departure point for free shuttle buses heading up to Lake Louise.

Lake Louise Visitor Centre

INFORMATION AND MAPS

We recommend that all hikers stop by the Lake Louise Visitor Centre (201 Village Road, 403/522-3833, ll.info@pc.gc.ca, open Oct.-May daily 9am-5pm and June-Sept. daily 9am-7pm) before embarking on any serious hiking in the area. Located in the village of Lake Louise beside Samson Mall on the corner of Village Road and Lake Louise Drive, this facility provides interpretive displays, current weather forecasts, reports on trail conditions and closures, and warnings concerning bear activity. It also has staff on hand to answer questions and recommend hikes suited to your ability. For pre-trip planning visit: www.pc.gc.ca/banff.

While the maps in this book cover each of the trails described, they are only designed to give you a general idea of trail location, course, and surrounding topography. It's always nice to have a more detailed map along to identify natural features and to help dispel confusion. Gem Trek produces the *Best of Lake Louise* (1:35,000) and *Lake Louise & Yoho* (1:50,000) maps; both are invaluable companions for your hiking adventures around the region. Both are sold at the Lake Louise Visitor Centre and at local retailers.

WHAT TO PACK

Even if you're planning a short walk, it is essential that you are prepared for changing weather. While the following recommendations will help you decide what to pack, the lighter you travel the more enjoyable your time in the wilderness will be.

While fit hikers can walk many of these trails in running shoes, you should always have sturdy walking shoes or hiking boots to cope with muddy, rocky and rooty tracks. If you have a new pair of shoes or boots, wear them once or twice before leaving home—just to make sure they are comfortable.

In summer, temperatures rarely drop below freezing, but you should prepare for a variety of weather conditions (especially if visiting in spring and fall) by dressing in layers. The best clothing is made from synthetic fabrics, which draw perspiration away from the body yet repel water. A breathable rain jacket should be carried regardless of the weather forecast. We always carry a warm hat (toque) and gloves throughout the year as insurance, but they are always necessary for longer hikes in spring and fall.

While not a necessity for most of these hikes, trekking poles significantly reduce stress on knees, especially on steep descents. They also decrease strain on feet and lower backs. While ski poles are better than nothing, serious hikers will want to invest in purpose-built telescopic, anti-shock, lightweight poles with flexible tips.

While natural sunlight is good for our health, too much can have adverse effects. This is especially relevant at higher elevations, where the air is thinner and cleaner, and the effects of UV exposure more pronounced. Always apply sunscreen, bring sunglasses, and some sort of sun hat.

Pack plenty of water on exposed hikes, such as to the summit of Fairview Mountain (pictured). Credit: Gordon Hobbs

It is essential to stay hydrated when hiking, especially at higher elevations. Due to the possible presence of *giardia* (see Dangers and Annoyances, page 16), use water purification devices or bring bottled water.

The walks and hikes detailed in this book do not require any special dietary considerations, although on longer walks it is important to keep your energy level up by eating high-octane carbohydrates, such as those found in energy bars. Remember to pack all garbage out. Do not leave anything behind—even apple cores.

Bug spray is a summer necessity. You can pick up the brands that are most effective at outdoor retailers and convenience stores throughout the park. A pre-packaged first aid kit can come in handy for longer hikes, but is not necessary for short walks. Even if you don't carry a complete kit, blister moleskin (available at most drugstores) or band-aids should be carried at all times. A spare plastic bag is handy for packing out garbage.

Carry everything in a lightweight daypack. The best daypacks are durable but lightweight, have padded shoulder straps and back panel. Waterproof pack covers and stuff sacks provide extra defense on rainy days.

SOME FINAL WORDS

Plan ahead. Choose trails you are in shape to handle. Allow time for unexpected weather and other events that might alter your schedule.

Stay on the trail, even if it means muddy boots. Leaving the trail creates parallel tracks and widens existing trails. Shortcutting switchbacks causes erosion.

Leave rocks, flowers, antlers, and other natural objects undisturbed. Never pick wildflowers or other plants.

Never feed, disturb, or harass wildlife. It is illegal, harmful to the animal's health, and alters their natural behaviour.

Take note of all signage on local trails.

Pack out all garbage. Carry plastic bags and, whenever possible, pack out litter that other, less considerate hikers have left behind.

Use washroom facilities provided at most trailheads.

Give horseback parties the right-of-way. If you encounter a horseback party, step well off the trail and stand still until it has passed.

Bow River Loop

This easy loop follows both banks of the Bow River and passes through the middle of the village of Lake Louise. It can be hiked in its entirety, or just one section.

NEED TO KNOW

LENGTH: 7-km (4.3-mile) loop

ELEVATION GAIN: Minimal

WALKING TIME: 2 hours roundtrip

RATING: Short hike

SEASON: May to October

INSIDER'S TIP

The section of trail along the east side of the river has the best views, while the south end of the loop offers the most solitude.

TRAILHEAD

Various points throughout Lake Louise Village, including a trailhead at the north end of the loop opposite the Station Restaurant, Sentinel Road (N51°25.713' W116°11.388').

Used by those on foot and bike to access various points in the village, the Bow River Loop also links a variety of village destinations, including the Station Restaurant, Samson Mall, the campground, and the Louise Creek and Tramline trails to Lake Louise. Interpretive signs along its length provide information on the Bow River ecosystem. If you are driving, we suggest starting this trail at the Station Restaurant, as parking is usually not a problem (there is limited parking at the trailhead, but just before the end of the road, on the river side, is a large parking lot).

It is possible to cut across bridges at Lake Louise Drive or the campground to shorten the total trail distance. For example, if you were to cross the Bow River at the pedestrian bridge beside the Station Restaurant, walk downstream and

The trail crosses the Pipestone River at its confluence with the Bow River.

cross the river again at Lake Louise Drive, then return to your starting point, total distance walked would be 1.6 kilometres (one mile); allow 30 minutes. Alternatively, the section of the trail downstream from the campground bridge traverses both sides of the river away from human habitation and takes around one hour to complete.

If you are walking the loop trail as designed, your destination will be your starting point, wherever that may be along the valley floor. If you are staying in the campground, use the trail to reach Samson Mall and enjoy hot drinks and a light meal at Laggan's Bakery, or a meal at the Station Restaurant.

BOW RIVER LOOP

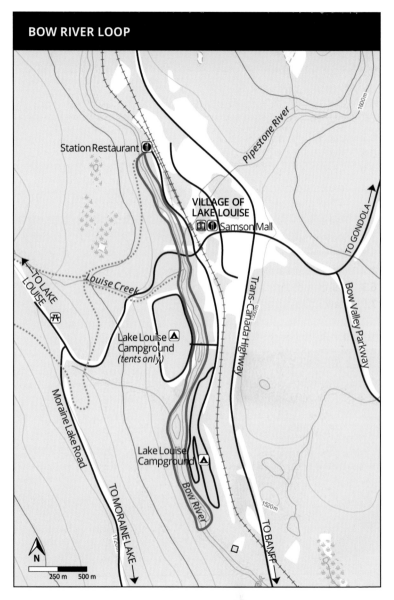

Station Restaurant

Pipestone River

VILLAGE OF
LAKE LOUISE

Samson Mall

TO GONDOLA →

Louise Creek

← TO LAKE LOUISE

Bow Valley Parkway

Lake Louise
Campground
(tents only)

Trans-Canada Highway

1520 m

Lake Louise
Campground

Moraine Lake Road

Bow River

TO MORAINE LAKE →

TO BANFF →

N

250 m   500 m

BOW RIVER LOOP TRAIL OUTLINE

This trail outline assumes you are beginning from the Station Restaurant.

0.0   Station Restaurant trailhead (elevation 1,530 m/5,020 ft).
—Cross Bow River Bridge.
0.1   Junction. Tramline ahead. Bow River Loop left.
0.8   Trail crosses Lake Louise Drive.
0.9   Junction. Louise Creek trail right. Bow River Loop ahead.
1.3   Trail crosses Louise Creek.
—Trail veers left toward Bow River and skirts electrified fence.
1.7   Trail crosses campground road.
3.5   South end of trail. Crosses the Bow River.
5.3   Trail crosses campground road.
6.2   Trail crosses Lake Louise Drive.
6.3   Trail crosses Pipestone River.
7.0   Station Restaurant trailhead.

The Station Restaurant is at the north end of the Bow River Loop.

Louise Creek

Assumed to follow the path taken by Tom Wilson in 1882, when he became the first European to lay eyes on Lake Louise, this trail is the quickest way to walk between the village and the lake—it's even slightly shorter than the road.

NEED TO KNOW

LENGTH: 2.8 km (1.7 miles) one-way

ELEVATION GAIN: 200 m (660 ft)

WALKING TIME: 1 hour one-way

RATING: Short hike

SEASON: Late May to October

INSIDER'S TIP

As there is no parking at the trailhead, start from Samson Mall, the campground, or the Station Restaurant, which are all linked by the Bow River Loop (see page 28).

TRAILHEAD

From Samson Mall walk beside Lake Louise Drive under the railway bridge. The trailhead is across the Bow River on the downstream side of the bridge (N51° 25.361′ W116° 10.894′).

Starting from a trail junction just below Lake Louise Drive after it crosses to the west side of the Bow River, the trail is within forest most of the way. After a few minutes of steady uphill, the trail crosses Louise Creek and then continues climbing to a pedestrian tunnel under Lake Louise Drive. It follows the Tramline trail for a short distance across Louise Creek and then veers left, resuming its uphill course. After just under one kilometre (0.6 miles), the trail again crosses Lake Louise Drive, and then after a short, steep, section merges with the Tramline trail for the final approach to Lake Louise.

At the end of the Louise Creek trail, where it reaches the parking lot, you're just five minutes from one of the world's most beautiful lakes. Walk through the parking lot and the lake presents itself in all its glory.

Louise Creek is a constant companion along this trail.

LOUISE CREEK TRAIL OUTLINE

0.0   Trailhead (elevation 1,530 m/5,020 ft).
         —Steady uphill.
0.4   Trail crosses Louise Creek.
0.7   Trail crosses under Lake Louise Drive.
1.3   Junction with Tramline trail. Continue straight ahead.
2.2   Trail crosses Lake Louise Drive.
2.4   Junction with Tramline trail. Veer right.
2.8   Lake Louise parking lot (elevation 1,730 m/5,680 ft).

Wild roses are common along the Louise Creek trail in early summer.

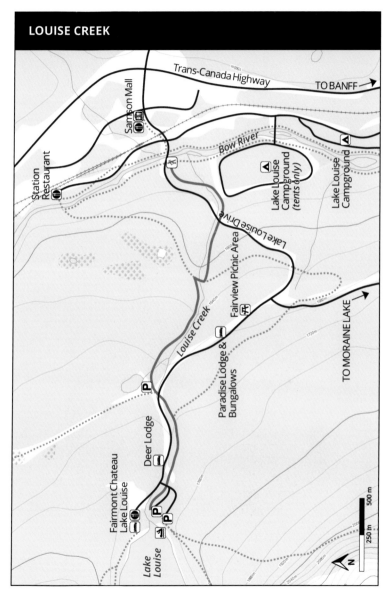

LOUISE CREEK

Trans-Canada Highway

TO BANFF

Samson Mall

Bow River

Station Restaurant

Lake Louise Campground (tents only)

Lake Louise Campground

Lake Louise Drive

Fairview Picnic Area

Louise Creek

Paradise Lodge & Bungalows

TO MORAINE LAKE

Deer Lodge

Fairmont Chateau Lake Louise

Lake Louise

N

250 m   500 m

Tramline

Longer than the Louise Creek trail, Tramline links the village to Lake Louise, following the grade of an abandoned tramline and creating an ideal alternative to driving up to the lake and adding to the traffic congestion.

NEED TO KNOW

LENGTH: 4.8 km (3 miles) one-way

ELEVATION GAIN: 200 m (660 ft)

WALKING TIME: 1.5 hours one-way

RATING: Short hike

SEASON: Late May to October

INSIDER'S TIP

Take the left fork up Louise Creek 1.6 km (1 mile) from the trailhead and you lessen the distance to Lake Louise by 1.7 km (1.1 miles) while still enjoying the viewpoint over the village.

TRAILHEAD

Parking area opposite the Station Restaurant, Sentinel Road, in the Village of Lake Louise (N51°25.713' W116°11.388').

Between 1913 and 1930, most visitors to Lake Louise arrived by train. Disembarking at the railway station (now a restaurant), guests would then jump aboard a tram running up to the lake on a narrow-gauge railway. While the rail line was removed many years ago, the wide, three-percent graded rail bed has been converted to a hiking trail.

The trail begins with a crossing of the Bow River and then climbs steadily to a viewpoint over the village. After one kilometre (0.6 miles) it crosses Louise Creek, which tumbles down from Lake Louise and then crosses firstly the main road up to the lake before doubling back toward the west, crossing Moraine Lake Road 3.1 kilometres from the trailhead. It parallels Lake Louise Drive and then Louise Creek to its end point.

The Tramline trail ends at the main Lake Louise parking lot. From this point, it's a short walk through the lot to the lake itself.

This trail follows the route of a narrow-gauge railway that transported visitors between the main CPR rail line and Lake Louise from 1913 to 1930.
Credit: Whyte Museum of the Canadian Rockies (v263-na-4864)

TRAMLINE

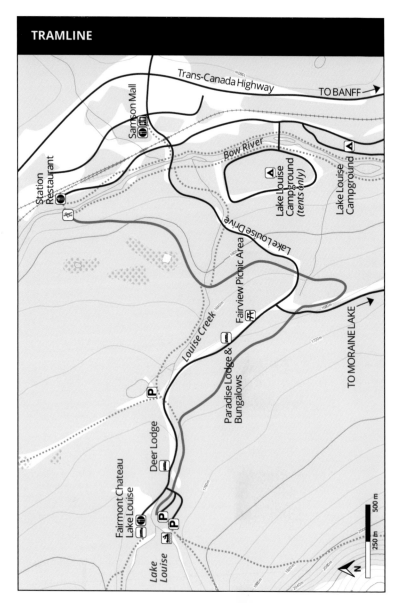

Trans-Canada Highway

TO BANFF →

Samson Mall

Bow River

Station Restaurant

Lake Louise Campground (tents only)

Lake Louise Campground

Lake Louise Drive

Fairview Picnic Area

Louise Creek

TO MORAINE LAKE

Paradise Lodge & Bungalows

Deer Lodge

Fairmont Chateau Lake Louise

Lake Louise

N

250 m   500 m

TRAMLINE TRAIL OUTLINE

0.0 Trailhead (elevation 1,530 m/5,020 ft).
  —Steady uphill on old railway bed.
1.0 Louise Creek crossing.
1.6 Junction. Louise Creek trail right. Tramline ahead.
2.4 Trail crosses Lake Louise Drive.
3.1 Trail crosses Moraine Lake Road.
4.4 Junction with Louise Creek trail. Stay left.
4.8 Lake Louise parking lot (elevation 1,730 m/5,680 ft).

Look for Indian paintbrush along open stretches of the Tramline trail.

Lake Louise Lakeshore

The Lake Louise Lakeshore trail is the busiest in the region, but even on a crowded summer's day, there are worse ways to spend an hour than strolling along this broad, flat trail with its ever-changing views of great peaks.

NEED TO KNOW

LENGTH: 1.9 km (1.2 miles) one-way

ELEVATION GAIN: Minimal

WALKING TIME: 30 minutes one-way

RATING: Easy walk

SEASON: Year-round

INSIDER'S TIP

Believe it or not, we have actually walked to the west end of Lake Louise and back on the very popular Lakeshore trail and not met another soul—but you'll need to rise early to enjoy the solitude.

TRAILHEAD

From in front of the Fairmont Chateau Lake Louise, follow paved trail north 200 metres (0.1 miles) to the official trailhead sign. (N51°25.044' W116°13.160').

From the trail sign at the northeast corner of Lake Louise, the wide trail follows along the north shoreline to where the silty meltwater from Victoria Glacier feeds into the lake. Away from the crowds surrounding the hotel, you can better appreciate the description by British mountaineer James Outram shortly after the turn of the 20th century: "At every season, every hour, it is wonderful.... As a gem of composition and of colouring it is perhaps unrivalled anywhere."

At the far end of the lake the trail climbs over a low rise and traverses beneath quartzite cliffs, which are often decorated by the colourful ropes of rock climbers. And if you sit down to have a snack, you'll undoubtedly be greeted by golden-mantled ground squirrels, chipmunks, Clark's nutcrackers and grey jays.

Back across the lake's distant shore, the Fairmont Chateau Lake Louise floats like the *Titanic*, with the ski-run-laced slopes of Whitehorn Mountain rising beyond. It's enough to make a person want to keep on hiking, which is possible along the Plain of Six Glaciers trail (see page 58).

Looking back down Lake Louise from beyond the end of the Lakeshore trail.

LAKE LOUISE LAKESHORE TRAIL OUTLINE

0.0   Trailhead (elevation 1,730 m/5,680 ft).
      —Easy walk along the north shoreline of Lake Louise.
1.9   West end of lake.

The back of the lake is a great place to view the combination of silt build-up and the famously turquoise water.

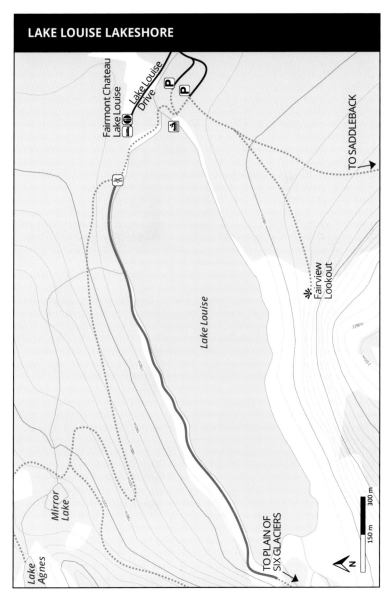

LAKE LOUISE LAKESHORE

Fairmont Chateau
Lake Louise

Lake Louise Drive

TO SADDLEBACK

Fairview
Lookout

Lake Louise

Mirror Lake

Lake Agnes

TO PLAIN OF SIX GLACIERS

300 m
150 m

N

Lake Agnes

Lake Agnes is hidden in a hanging valley high above Lake Louise. In addition to its own charms, which include a tea house and the lake, the nearby Beehives provide breathtaking views of Lake Louise and a broad stretch of the Bow Valley.

NEED TO KNOW

LENGTH: 3.5 km (2.2 miles) one-way

ELEVATION GAIN: 405 m (1,330 ft)

WALKING TIME: 1 hour one-way

RATING: Short hike

SEASON: June to early October

TRAILHEAD

Follow the paved lakeshore trail in front of Fairmont Chateau Lake Louise north 200 metres (0.1 miles) to the Lake Agnes trail, leading uphill to the right (N51°25.044' W116°13.160').

INSIDER'S TIP

We recommend continuing along the north shore of Lake Agnes to its boulder-strewn western end, only 800 metres (0.5 miles) beyond the tea house, for better lake views and, in mid-September, a wonderful display of golden larch.

The first half hour from the shore of Lake Louise follows a broad, moderately graded trail through dense subalpine forest. At 1.7 kilometres (0.9 miles) the first switchback marks a break in the trees where you have a clear view down to the pale turquoise waters of Lake Louise.

Another 900 metres (0.6 miles) brings you to Mirror Lake—a tiny sink lake that takes its name from its round looking-glass appearance. The dark, layered cliffs of Big Beehive loom above, and, in the gap to the right, the roof of Lake Agnes Tea House is barely visible.

Mirror Lake and the Big Beehive

By taking the Plain of Six Glaciers Highline trail to the left at the Mirror Lake junction, you can make a direct ascent to Lake Agnes via a steep trail that traverses the rockslide beneath Big Beehive. (This short cut branches right from the Highline trail 150 metres/0.1 miles beyond this junction.) But if this steep trail is wet, icy or snowy, avoid it and follow the traditional route that branches right at Mirror Lake (it's only slightly longer).

Regardless of which option you choose, the journey to Lake Agnes is completed on one of two steep, wooden staircases that surmount a cliff band beside the waterfall created by the lake's outlet stream.

Arriving at the narrow opening where Lake Agnes tumbles from its basin, the entire length of the lake suddenly appears, stretching westward to a jagged backdrop created by Mounts Whyte (2,983 metres/9,790 feet) and Niblock (2,976 metres/9,760 feet). The tea house sits atop the cliff on the north side of the outlet stream, overlooking the lake.

The original **Lake Agnes Tea House** was constructed shortly after the turn of the 20th century. The present-day version was built in 1981. It serves refreshments and light snacks daily 8am to 5pm from early June to early October. While its covered porch is a relaxing place to sit and admire the view, it is usually a very busy place. It is cash only (no debit or credit cards).

OPTIONS

The most popular short hikes beyond Lake Agnes are to the **Little Beehive** (see page 50) and the **Big Beehive** (see page 54).

The **Lake Agnes-Plain of Six Glaciers Circuit** is a 14.5-kilometre (nine-mile) hike that combines the two most popular trails from Lake Louise. Cross the Big Beehive's summit ridge at the viewpoint trail junction and follow a steep trail down the south side. Reaching the Highline trail running up-valley from Mirror Lake, turn right and follow the Highline trail for 2.2 kilometres (1.4 miles) to an intersection with the Plain of Six Glaciers trail, from where it's a further 1.4 kilometres (0.9 miles) to the Plain of Six Glaciers Tea House. See Plain of Six Glaciers trail, page 58.

LAKE AGNES

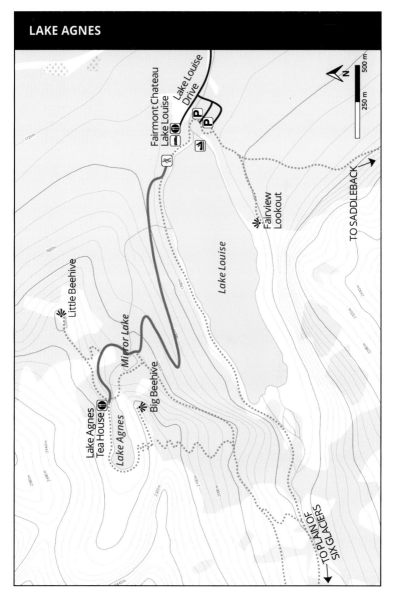

N

250 m 500 m

Fairmont Chateau
Lake Louise

Lake Louise
Drive

P
P

Fairview
Lookout

Lake Louise

TO SADDLEBACK

Little Beehive

Mirror Lake

Big Beehive

Lake Agnes
Tea House

Lake Agnes

TO PLAIN OF
SIX GLACIERS

LAKE AGNES TRAIL OUTLINE

0.0 Trailhead (elevation 1,730 m/5,680 ft).
   —Steady uphill on broad track.
1.7 Switchback. View to Lake Louise.
2.5 Junction. Horse trail intersects from right.
2.6 Mirror Lake. Junction. Highline trail left. Lake Agnes right.
   —Switchbacks begin.
3.2 Junction. Little Beehive shortcut right. Lake Agnes ahead.
3.5 Lake Agnes and Tea House (elevation 2,135 m/7,000 ft).

Lake Agnes Tea House

Lake Agnes in mid-September.

Little Beehive

The Little Beehive is the most popular short hike beyond Lake Agnes. Though slightly lower than the nearby Big Beehive, it provides better views of both Lake Louise and the Bow Valley, and you won't work quite as hard to get there.

NEED TO KNOW

LENGTH: 4.5 km (2.8 miles) one-way

ELEVATION GAIN: 495 m (1,620 ft)

WALKING TIME: 1.5 hours one-way

RATING: Moderate hike

SEASON: Mid-June to early October

INSIDER'S TIP

To fully appreciate the sweeping mountain views from Little Beehive, bring a map to help identify the landmark peaks.

TRAILHEAD

Follow the paved lakeshore trail in front of Fairmont Chateau Lake Louise north 200 metres (0.1 miles) to the Lake Agnes trail, leading uphill to the right (N51°25.044' W116°13.160').

Starting from the front of the Fairmont Chateau Lake Louise, the initial 3.5 kilometres (2.2 miles) and 405 metres (1,330 feet) of elevation gain are along the Lake Agnes trail (see page 44).

After reaching the tea house, continue along the shoreline of Lake Agnes for 50 metres (160 feet) then take the trail branching uphill to the right. It climbs steadily to the northeast through alpine fir and larch and across avalanche slopes. Along the way there are a number of stunning rocky viewpoints overlooking Lake Louise, the hanging valley containing Lake Agnes, and Mount Aberdeen and the glacier-crowned peaks of Mounts Lefroy and Victoria. Stands of larch become thicker as you climb, making this a very rewarding trip in the last two weeks of September when their needles turn to gold.

The trail ends one kilometre (0.6 miles) from Lake Agnes at the 2,225-metre-high (7,300-foot) Little Beehive summit and the concrete foundation of an old fire lookout cabin. Views are quite impressive, including a panorama of the Bow Valley that stretches from the mountains near the headwaters of the Bow River to the peaks surrounding the town of Banff to the south. Across the way, the Pipestone River stretches north into some of the wildest country in Banff National Park.

Looking back across Mirror Lake to Mount Aberdeen.

OPTION

Returning toward Lake Agnes, a short cut spurs downhill 500 metres (0.3 miles) from the Little Beehive, rejoining the Lake Agnes trail 3.2 kilometres (two miles) from the main trailhead.

LITTLE BEEHIVE

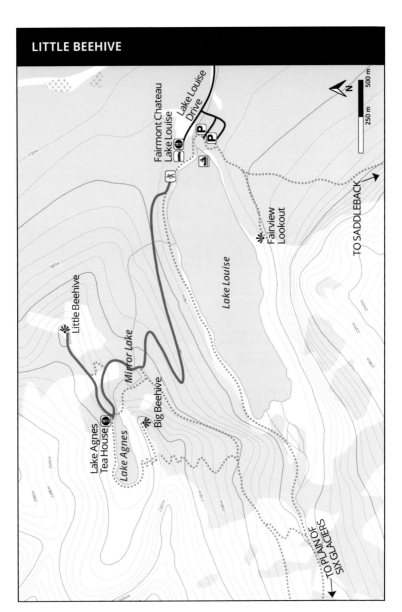

LITTLE BEEHIVE TRAIL OUTLINE

0.0   Trailhead (elevation 1,730 m/5,680 ft).
          —Steady uphill on broad track.
1.7   Switchback. View to Lake Louise.
2.5   Junction. Horse trail intersects from right.
2.6   Mirror Lake. Junction. Highline trail left. Lake Agnes right.
          —Switchbacks begin.
3.2   Junction. Little Beehive shortcut right. Lake Agnes ahead.
3.5   Lake Agnes and Tea House.
3.6   Junction. Big Beehive ahead. Little Beehive right.
4.0   Junction. Little Beehive ahead. Shortcut to Lake Agnes trail right.
4.5   Little Beehive (elevation 2,225 m/7,300 ft).

The foundations of a fire lookout built on the Little Beehive in 1941.

Big Beehive

In addition to Little Beehive, another popular trip beyond Lake Agnes Tea House is the hike to the 2,255-metre-high (7,400-foot) summit of Big Beehive, from where views of Lake Louise are somewhat limited, but the panorama of the surrounding mountainscape is well worth the effort.

NEED TO KNOW

LENGTH: 5.1 km (3.2 miles) one-way

ELEVATION GAIN: 520 m (1,710 ft)

WALKING TIME: 1.5 to 2 hours one-way

RATING: Moderate hike

SEASON: Mid-June to early October

INSIDER'S TIP

From the 4.8-km (three-mile) junction, descend toward Lake Louise and when you reach the Highline trail go left toward Mirror Lake and you quickly reach a section of trail with stunning views of Lake Louise.

TRAILHEAD

Follow the paved lakeshore trail in front of Fairmont Chateau Lake Louise north 200 metres (0.1 miles) to the Lake Agnes trail, leading uphill to the right (N51°25.044' W116°13.160').

As with the Little Beehive, to reach the Big Beehive, you must first hike up the Lake Agnes trail (see page 44), 3.5 kilometres (2.2 miles) and 405 metres (1,330 feet) of elevation gain from Lake Louise. Once at the Lake Agnes Tea House, continue on the narrow trail along the north side of Lake Agnes. The trail then continues around the far end of the lake and climbs steep switchbacks to a junction on the Big Beehive summit ridge. Traverse eastward (left) along the rocky, lightly forested ridge to a log gazebo shelter on the northeast edge of the promontory.

Though somewhat obscured by trees, there are views over the Bow Valley and down to Lake Louise, 520 metres (1,710 feet) below. Across Lake Louise is Fairview Mountain (2,745 metres/9,000 feet). Views also extend up the lake to Mount Lefroy and northeast to Lake Louise ski resort. Do not attempt to shortcut down from the gazebo viewpoint in any direction; there are dangerous cliffs on all sides. Return along the ridge the way you came.

OPTION

Backtrack to where the trail from Lake Agnes first reaches the top of the ridge and a trail descends steeply to the south toward Lake Louise. After one kilometre (0.6 miles) it ends at the **Highline Trail** that links Mirror Lake to the Plain of Six Glaciers trail. The shortest way back to the original trailhead is to take the left option, which reaches Mirror Lake in 0.9 kilometres (0.5 miles) and includes a section of trail with open views down the lake to the Fairmont Chateau Lake Louise.

Hikers looking for a full day's outing can take the right option at the Highline trail junction to include the Plain of Six Glaciers trail (see page 58) in their itinerary. From the junction it is 3.6 kilometres (2.2 miles) to the Plain of Six Glaciers Tea House and the total distance of this circuit is 14.5 kilometres (nine miles); allow around five hours, and bring cash for tea house stops.

BIG BEEHIVE TRAIL OUTLINE

0.0 Trailhead (elevation 1,730 m/5,680 ft).
    —Steady uphill on broad track.
1.7 Switchback. View to Lake Louise.
2.5 Junction. Horse trail intersects from right.
2.6 Mirror Lake. Junction. Highline trail left. Lake Agnes right.
    —Switchbacks begin.
3.2 Junction. Little Beehive shortcut right. Lake Agnes ahead.
3.5 Lake Agnes and Tea House.
4.1 West end of Lake Agnes.
    —Steep switchbacks.
4.8 Junction. Big Beehive left. Highline trail ahead.
5.1 Big Beehive (elevation 2,255 m/7,400 ft).

Looking down to the Fairmont Chateau Lake Louise from the Highline trail.

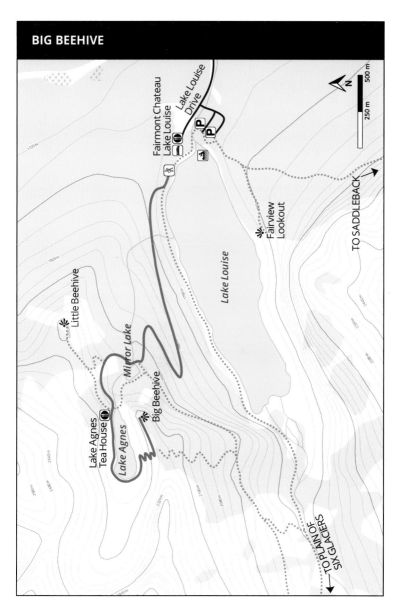

BIG BEEHIVE

Fairmont Chateau
Lake Louise

Lake Louise Drive

Fairview Lookout

Lake Louise

TO SADDLEBACK

Little Beehive

Mirror Lake

Big Beehive

Lake Agnes Tea House

Lake Agnes

TO PLAIN OF SIX GLACIERS

N

250 m   500 m

Plain of Six Glaciers

This trail leads into the Canadian Rockies' most famous postcard view beneath the glacier-capped summits of Mounts Victoria and Lefroy. As a bonus, you can stop for refreshments at a backcountry tea house.

NEED TO KNOW

LENGTH: 5.5 km (3.4 miles) one-way

ELEVATION GAIN: 360 m (1,180 ft)

WALKING TIME: 1.5-2 hours one-way

RATING: Moderate hike

SEASON: Mid-June to early October

INSIDER'S TIP

Bring plenty of drinking water as the route to the tea house is exposed, especially under the heat of the midday sun.

TRAILHEAD

From in front of the Fairmont Chateau Lake Louise, follow the paved trail north 200 metres (0.1 miles) to the official trailhead sign. (N51°25.044' W116°13.160').

To reach Plain of Six Glaciers, follow the busy Lake Louise Lakeshore trail (see page 40) to the far end of Lake Louise. Beyond the lake's silty inlet, the crowds thin as the trail climbs steadily through subalpine forest and across the occasional avalanche path. Eventually it emerges into a landscape scoured by the Victoria Glacier, where views open to Mounts Victoria and Lefroy.

After passing the intersection with the Highline trail from Mirror Lake and the Big Beehive, you ascend along the edge of old glacial moraines. A final series of steep switchbacks lead up through a band of alpine fir and larch to the tea house.

The **Plain of Six Glaciers Tea House** was constructed by the Canadian Pacific Railway in the mid-1920s. Refreshments and light snacks are served daily 9am to 5pm early June to early October (in early June,

Plain of Six Glaciers Tea House

check with the Lake Louise Visitor Centre as sometimes a lingering snowpack delays the opening). The tea house verandah is an ideal vantage point for watching the frequent avalanches thundering off Mounts Lefroy and Victoria in the early summer. If the tea house is overflowing with visitors, as it often is in the middle of the day, you can relax in the clearing below the tea house and scan the nearby boulder-field for hoary marmots and pikas.

OPTION

The trail continues up-valley beyond the tea house for another 1.3 kilometres (0.8 miles) to the **Abbot Pass Viewpoint** (allow 20 minutes each way). Along the way it traverses the crest of a lateral moraine—a steep ridge of debris formed during the last advance of the Victoria Glacier, which reached its zenith during the mid-1800s. Today it provides an excellent viewpoint for the rock and boulder-covered ice of the Victoria Glacier below.

Beyond the moraine, the trail fizzles out on a steep talus slope. While this slope is a rather precarious resting spot, it is the best viewpoint for Abbot Pass (2,922 metres/9,590 feet) between the towering summits of Mount Victoria and Mount Lefroy and the Abbot Pass Hut—a substantial stone structure constructed by Swiss guides in 1922 as an overnight shelter for mountaineers. Today it is operated by the Alpine Club of Canada and is Canada's highest National Historic Site.

The steep, ice-filled couloir rising from the Victoria Glacier to the pass is known as "The Death Trap", so-named by early mountaineers because avalanches frequently fall into it from the cliffs above. (Don't even dream of heading in that direction unless you are an experienced, well-equipped mountaineer and have checked with Parks Canada about current route conditions.)

Heading up to the Abbot Pass Viewpoint.

PLAIN OF SIX GLACIERS

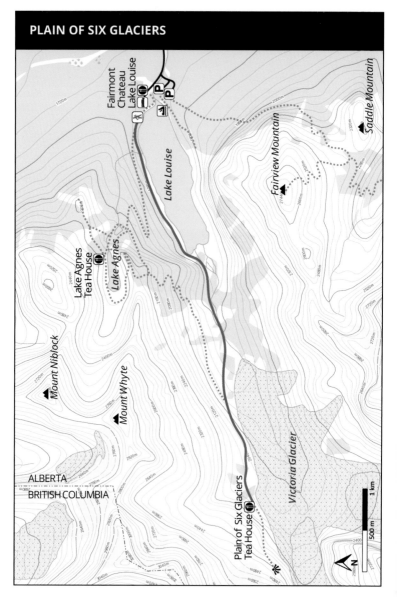

Fairmont Chateau Lake Louise

Lake Louise

Saddle Mountain

Fairview Mountain

Lake Agnes Tea House

Lake Agnes

Mount Niblock

Mount Whyte

Victoria Glacier

ALBERTA

BRITISH COLUMBIA

Plain of Six Glaciers Tea House

1 km

500 m

N

PLAIN OF SIX GLACIERS TRAIL OUTLINE

0.0 Trailhead (elevation 1,730 m/5,680 ft).
—Follow Lake Louise Lakeshore trail.
1.9 West end of Lake Louise.
2.4 Steady climb begins.
3.3 Junction. Big Beehive shortcut right. Plain of Six Glaciers ahead.
4.1 Junction. Highline trail and Big Beehive right. Plain of Six Glaciers ahead.
5.5 Plain of Six Glaciers Tea House (elevation 2,090 m/6,860 ft).

The river flowing into Lake Louise is filled with silt from melting glaciers.

Fairview Lookout

This short, moderately steep hike from the lakeshore near the Fairmont Chateau Lake Louise takes you through the cool Engelmann spruce-alpine fir forest to an observation platform overlooking the east end of the lake and the Chateau.

NEED TO KNOW

LENGTH: 1 km (0.6 miles) one-way

ELEVATION GAIN: 140 m (455 ft)

WALKING TIME: 30 minutes one-way

RATING: Short hike

SEASON: June to October

INSIDER'S TIP

Although a faint trail leads downhill toward the lake from the viewpoint, don't take it—this route was decommissioned many years ago and can be extremely muddy.

TRAILHEAD

Exhibit area between the lake's outlet bridge and the Lake Louise Boathouse (N51°24.969' W116°12.964').

From the shoreline viewpoint near the boathouse, follow the Saddleback trail. After 300 metres (0.2 miles), branch right onto the Fairview trail. The remainder of the hike follows a smooth track, climbing steadily through mossy forest to the viewing platform.

This is one of the best viewpoints for the Fairmont Chateau Lake Louise and the busy east end of the lake. The Chateau sits atop a glacial moraine that acted as a natural dam to create the lake many thousands of years ago.

From this height, you can appreciate the startling turquoise colour of Lake Louise, which isn't as obvious from the shoreline. The colour is created by the glaciers at the head of the valley. These bodies of ice are continually grinding away at bedrock, and their meltwaters are thick with very fine silt, also know as glacial flour. The material is so fine that much of it remains suspended in the water long after it pours into the lake from the main tributary stream at the west end. When the sun strikes these particles all colours of the spectrum are absorbed except blue and green, which are reflected.

Though the lake is relatively small— only two kilometres (1.2 miles) long and less than 500 metres (0.3 miles) wide—it is 70 metres (230 feet) at its maximum depth, making it one of the Canadian Rockies' deepest lakes.

This 1920 photo from Fairview Lookout shows the original wooden chalet and, to the left, the first phase of the Chateau Lake Louise as we know it today. Credit: Whyte Museum of the Canadian Rockies (v263-na-4860)

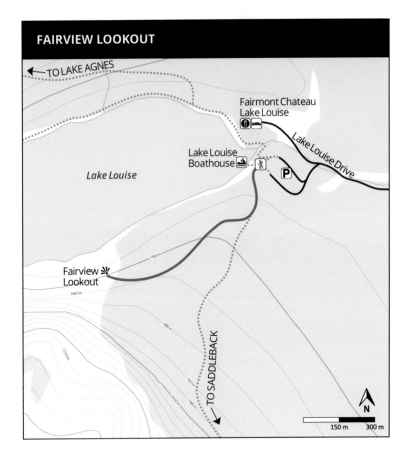

FAIRVIEW LOOKOUT TRAIL OUTLINE

0.0 Trailhead (elevation 1,730 m/5,680 ft).

0.3 Junction. Saddleback trail ahead. Fairview Lookout right.
  —Steady climb through forest.

1.0 Fairview Lookout (elevation 1,870 m/6,140 ft).

Saddleback

The hike to Saddleback is the steepest and most demanding hike from the shores of Lake Louise. It is also one of the most rewarding, boasting the best viewpoint for Mount Temple's massive north face, wildflower meadows, and stands of golden-needled alpine larch in late September.

NEED TO KNOW

LENGTH: 3.7 km (2.3 miles) one-way

ELEVATION GAIN: 600 m (1,965 ft)

WALKING TIME: 1.5 to 2 hours one-way

RATING: Day trip

SEASON: Late June to early October

INSIDER'S TIP

If you hike to the summit of Fairview Mountain, do not attempt to shortcut directly down to Lake Louise. This is a very dangerous option. Return the way you came.

TRAILHEAD

Exhibit area between the lake's outlet bridge and the Lake Louise Boathouse (N51°24.969' W116°12.964').

In its early stages the trail climbs steadily through the forest. At the end of the first one kilometre (0.6 miles) it crosses a major avalanche path on Fairview's northeast slopes, where you have a view back to the Chateau and distant Mount Hector. Farther along, the trail angles up to the southwest and begins the final steep, switchbacking ascent to the pass.

Views improve just below the summit, stretching down the length of the Bow Valley to the mountains near the town of Banff. You also pass through a stand of unusually large and very old, alpine larch (core samples from similar trees in nearby Larch Valley reveal ages of more than 400 years).

Saddleback is a pleasant upland meadow where buttercups, western anemone, alpine speedwell and many other wildflowers bloom in early summer. The towering north wall of Mount Temple (3,544 metres/11,630 feet), the third highest mountain in Banff National Park, dominates the view south of the pass. The best view of Mount Temple, looming over tiny Lake Annette and Paradise Valley, is found a short distance southeast of the trail along the summit ridge. Follow a faint path through scrub alpine fir to an open promontory overlooking Sheol Valley.

OPTION

With the glacier-crowned summits of Mount Victoria, Mount Temple and Sheol Mountain close by, and the turquoise waters of Lake Louise 1,000 vertical metres (3,280 feet) below, the 2,745-metre (9,010-foot) summit of **Fairview Mountain** offers a true alpine experience. The peak is arguably the highest trail-accessible point in the mountain parks, though the 1.3-kilometre (0.8-mile) track scratched up its rocky slope many decades ago has largely disappeared. Follow faint trail northwest from Saddleback summit to begin the ascent. Continue upwards on often vague, switchbacking track, or simply scramble over loose rock towards the obvious summit. (You may have to skirt snowbanks early in the season.)

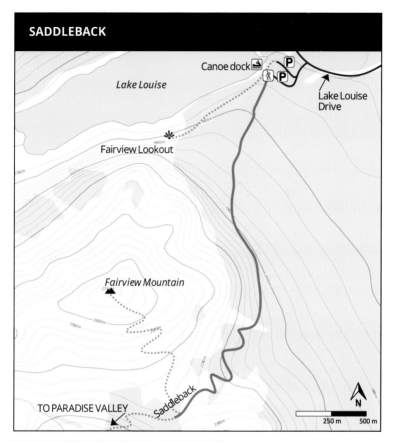

SADDLEBACK

Lake Louise

Canoe dock

P
P

Lake Louise Drive

Fairview Lookout

1840 m

Fairview Mountain

TO PARADISE VALLEY   Saddleback

N

250 m   500 m

SADDLEBACK TRAIL OUTLINE

0.0 Trailhead (elevation 1,730 m/5,680 ft).

0.3 Junction. Fairview Lookout right. Saddleback ahead.

0.4 Junction. Moraine Lake-Paradise Valley left. Saddleback ahead.

1.1 Avalanche path.
      —Moderate to steep uphill begins.

2.7 Alpine larch stands.

3.7 Saddleback summit (elevation 2,330 m/7,640 ft).

Paradise Valley

A 10.3-kilometre (6.4-mile) trail runs up Paradise Valley from Moraine Lake Road to the Giant Steps cascades. While it's possible to hike to the Giant Steps and back in a long day, most opt for a more scenic objective, Lake Annette, beneath the imposing north wall of Mount Temple.

NEED TO KNOW

LENGTH: 10.3 km (6.4 miles) one-way

ELEVATION GAIN: 385 m (1,250 ft)

WALKING TIME: 3 hours one-way

RATING: Day trip

SEASON: Mid-June to early October

INSIDER'S TIP

Travel in Paradise Valley may require a group of four people if special restrictions concerning grizzly bears are in place, so check with the Lake Louise Visitor Centre before heading out.

TRAILHEAD

Follow Moraine Lake Road 2.5 km (1.5 miles) from Lake Louise Drive to the Paradise Valley parking area (N51°23.763' W116°10.306').

When Walter Wilcox and his companions climbed to the summit of Mitre Pass from Lake Louise in 1894, they looked into "a valley of surpassing beauty, wide and beautiful, with alternating open meadows and rich forests." They named it Paradise.

The first three kilometres (1.9 miles) of trail are forest-enclosed, but at the first Paradise Creek bridge, views open to Mount Temple. In another 500 metres (0.3 miles), you cross back to the northwest side of the creek and pass the Sheol Valley-Saddleback junction. At km 5.1 (mile 3.2), the trail crosses the creek once more followed by a short but strenuous ascent to Lake Annette.

Lake Annette's rocky surroundings are typical of many subalpine tarns, but its backdrop is extraordinary—the ice-capped, 1,200-metre (3,940-foot) north face of Mount Temple. This wall is one of the most difficult ascents in North America and remained unclimbed until 1966. And if you see one of the massive avalanches that sweep the face, you will understand one reason why.

Lake Annette

The trail continues west from Lake Annette, climbing through stands of alpine larch at the base of Mount Temple. Even if you don't plan on hiking to the Giant Steps, it's worthwhile continuing another 15 minutes or so beyond the lake to the trail's summit atop a major rockslide. Here views open to the valley headwall—Hungabee Mountain, Ringrose Peak, and Horseshoe Glacier—scenery that is blithely ignored by the marmots and pikas inhabiting the surrounding boulder field.

Nearly two kilometres (1.2 miles) beyond the trail summit, you reach a cutoff trail to the Giant Steps. This trail descends to a bridge over Paradise Creek then angles directly across the valley to the Giant Steps and Paradise Valley Campground. Sections of old trail loop further up-valley to the head of the Horseshoe Meadows, but there seems little reason to hike this slightly longer route.

Nearing the Giant Steps, you pass the branch trail to Paradise Valley Campground. Stay right and, just 200 metres (0.1 miles) beyond this junction, reach the Giant Steps—a remarkable staircase waterfall on the north fork of Paradise Creek. The falls have been photographed many times over the years, but some of the earliest images were made by members of the Alpine Club of Canada, who held their second annual camp here in 1907.

OPTION

At the 8.4-kilometre (5.2-mile) junction, take the left branch that continues along the southeast side of the valley. In another 400 metres (0.3 miles), you reach Sentinel Pass junction. The pass lies a very steep and rocky 2.3 kilometres (1.4 miles) up to the left. Most hikers find it less strenuous to climb to **Sentinel Pass** from Moraine Lake and then descend to Paradise Valley. This 17-kilometre (10.6-mile) traverse between Moraine Lake and the Paradise Valley trailhead is fairly popular with parties who can arrange transportation. (See Larch Valley trail, page 80.)

OTHER NOTES

When the Moraine Lake Road is closed due to a full parking lot at Moraine Lake, the closure applies to all traffic on the road and therefore it is not possible to reach the Paradise Valley trailhead. Plan on arriving before 8am to access to the Paradise Valley trailhead.

Giant Steps

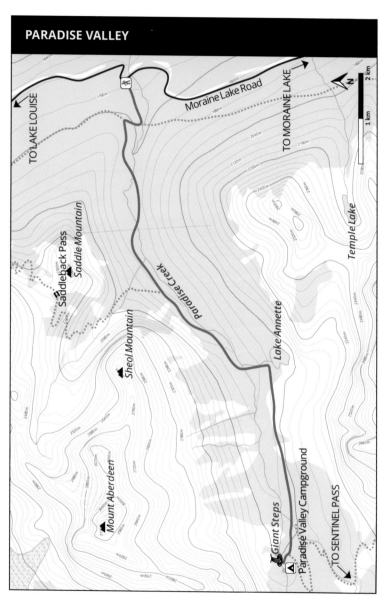

PARADISE VALLEY

TO LAKE LOUISE

Moraine Lake Road

TO MORAINE LAKE

N

1 km   2 km

Saddleback Pass

Saddle Mountain

Sheol Mountain

Paradise Creek

Lake Annette

Temple Lake

Mount Aberdeen

Giant Steps

Paradise Valley Campground

TO SENTINEL PASS

PARADISE VALLEY TRAIL OUTLINE

0.0 Trailhead (elevation 1,720 m/5,640 ft).
0.1 Junction. Paradise Valley left.
1.1 Junction. Moraine Lake left. Paradise Valley right.
1.3 Junction. Lake Louise ahead (4 km/2.5 miles). Paradise Valley left.
3.4 Paradise Creek bridge.
3.9 Paradise Creek bridge.
4.2 Junction. Saddleback via Sheol Valley right 4.1 km (2.5 miles).
5.1 Paradise Creek bridge.
5.7 Lake Annette (elevation 1,965 m/6,450 ft).
6.5 Trail summit (elevation 2,105 m/6,910 ft).
8.4 Junction. Sentinel Pass left 2.7 km (1.7 miles). Giant Steps right.
9.1 Paradise Creek bridge, junction. Horseshoe Meadows left. Giant Steps ahead.
9.2 Junction. Horseshoe Meadows left. Giant Steps ahead.
9.5 Junction. Horseshoe Meadows left. Giant Steps ahead.
10.1 Junction. Paradise Valley Campground left 0.2 km (0.1 miles). Giant Steps ahead.
10.3 Giant Steps (elevation 2,000 m/6,560 ft).

The first crossing of Paradise Creek is 3.4 kilometres from the trailhead.

Moraine Lakeshore

In the heart of the Valley of the Ten Peaks, this is an easy walk along the shoreline of one of the world's most photographed lakes. Be sure to also include the short climb to the top of the Rockpile, which starts at a bridge over Moraine Creek beside the public washrooms.

NEED TO KNOW

LENGTH: 1.2 km (0.7 miles) one way

ELEVATION GAIN: Minimal

WALKING TIME: 20 minutes one way

RATING: Easy walk

SEASON: Late May to mid-October

INSIDER'S TIP

The Moraine Lake area is very popular. Plan on arriving before 9am (and before 8am in July and August) to ensure a parking spot. When the parking lot is full, Moraine Lake Road is closed.

TRAILHEAD

Follow the Moraine Lake Road 12.5 km (7.5 miles) to the parking area at Moraine Lake. Walk to the lakeshore and the trail sign below the lodge (N51°19.673' W116°10.899').

In 1899, Walter Wilcox and Ross Peacock set out to explore the lower reaches of "Desolation Valley," which Wilcox had surveyed from the summit of Mount Temple five years earlier. After a hard bushwhack into the valley, Wilcox came to a "massive pile of stones" blocking the way ahead. He climbed to the top and, behold, "there lay before me one of the most beautiful lakes that I have ever seen."

Today, thousands climb the **Rockpile**, Wilcox's viewpoint, to photograph the classic view of the lake. To do so, use the trail starting from beside the public washrooms. However, the trail down its northwest shoreline, away from the crowds milling about the parking lot, lodge and viewpoint, provides a different perspective for what many visitors feel is one of the most beautiful lakes they've ever seen.

From the trail sign just below Moraine Lake Lodge, continue on the lakeside trail. The trail remains flat and close to the shoreline all the way to the lake's inlet at its southwest end. Along the way, you have continuous views across the lake to the rugged summits of the first five of the Ten Peaks rising from its eastern shore. Most impressive is Peak #1, Mount Fay, with its prominent summit glacier.

Looking back to the Rockpile from the Moraine Lakeshore trail.

Moraine Lake from the base of the Rockpile.

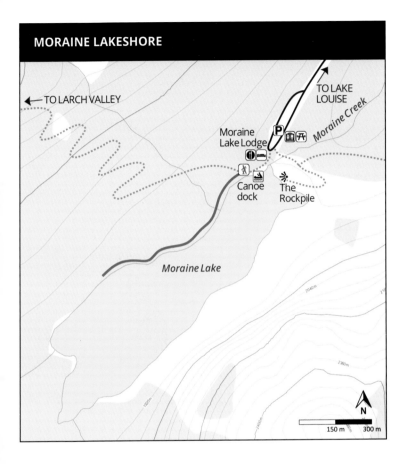

MORAINE LAKESHORE

MORAINE LAKESHORE

TO LARCH VALLEY

TO LAKE LOUISE

Moraine Creek

Moraine Lake Lodge

Canoe dock

The Rockpile

Moraine Lake

N

150 m   300 m

MORAINE LAKESHORE TRAIL OUTLINE

0.0 Trailhead (elevation 1,887 m/6,190 ft).
0.2 Junction. Larch Valley-Eiffel Lake right. Stay left.
        —Easy walk along northwest shoreline of Moraine Lake.
1.2 End of trail.

Larch Valley

This meadowland above Moraine Lake, with its dense stands of alpine larch and panoramic overview of the Ten Peaks, is exquisite. And above the valley, amid stark pinnacles of rock, is Sentinel Pass—the highest point reached by a major trail in the mountain national parks.

NEED TO KNOW

LENGTH: 4.5 km (2.8 miles) one-way

ELEVATION GAIN: 550 m (1,800 ft)

WALKING TIME: 1.5 to 2 hours one-way

RATING: Moderate hike

SEASON: Late June to early October

INSIDER'S TIP

Although the trail enters Larch Valley after 2.4 kilometres (1.5 miles), it is well worth continuing to the end of the trail at Upper Minnestimma Lake, where the very best views unfold back across to the Valley of the Ten Peaks.

TRAILHEAD

Follow the Moraine Lake Road 12.5 kilometres (7.5 miles) to the parking area at Moraine Lake. Walk to the lakeshore and the trail sign below the lodge (N51°19.673' W116°10.899').

From Moraine Lake the trail climbs through a forest of Engelmann spruce and alpine fir, following a steadily ascending series of switchbacks much of the way. At kilometre 2.4 (mile 1.5) the trail branches right from the Eiffel Lake trail and immediately enters the lower meadows of Larch Valley.

This high valley is the main focus for most hikers who walk the trail, and in late September, when alpine larch needles have turned to gold, it is one of the most visited trails in the Rockies. In mid-summer, however, the larch needles are a pale green and the meadows are carpeted with wildflowers.

Most hikers will want to explore the entire vale to Upper Minnestimma Lake, which lies above the last trees at the foot of Sentinel Pass. Looking south from this high meadowland, the heavily-glaciated Valley of the Ten Peaks stretch across the horizon, providing one of the most striking panoramas in the Canadian Rockies.

OPTION

Between the rugged walls of Pinnacle Mountain on the left and Mount Temple on the right, is the 2,611-metre (8,570-foot) summit of **Sentinel Pass**. After passing the uppermost Minnestimma Lake, the trail begins a switchbacking climb of the steep, open slope leading to the pass—a vertical rise of nearly 200 metres (660 feet) in 1.3 kilometres (0.8 miles) that weeds out most Larch Valley hikers.

The rock formations surrounding Sentinel Pass lie nearly horizontal, and erosion of these layers has created the weird spires immediately north of the summit. The pass receives its name from these towers, the tallest of which is called the Grand Sentinel.

The pass was first ascended in 1894 by Samuel Allen and Yandell Henderson, members of a group of American mountain climbers

The sentinels of Sentinel Pass | Credit: Chuck O'Callaghan

exploring the Lake Louise region. A few days later Allen returned to the pass with Walter Wilcox and Louis Frissell and climbed Mount Temple (3,544 metres/11,630 feet).

Strong hikers who have arranged transportation between trailheads at Moraine Lake and Paradise Valley can continue north over Sentinel Pass and descend into Paradise Valley (see page 70). The 2.7-kilometre (1.7-mile) trail down the north slope of the pass is extremely steep. Trail-obscuring snowfields often linger into late summer near the bottom of the slope. The trail should be avoided entirely when the boulders near Sentinel Pass are snow or ice-covered. Total distance from Moraine Lake to the Paradise Valley trailhead is 17 kilometres (10.6 miles).

OTHER NOTES

Travel on the Larch Valley trail may require a group of four people hiking in close proximity to one another if special restrictions concerning grizzly bears are in place.

The Moraine Lake area is very popular. Plan on arriving before 9am (and before 8am in July and August) to ensure a parking spot. When the parking lot is full, Moraine Lake Road is closed.

Look for marmots sunning themselves on rocks in Larch Valley.

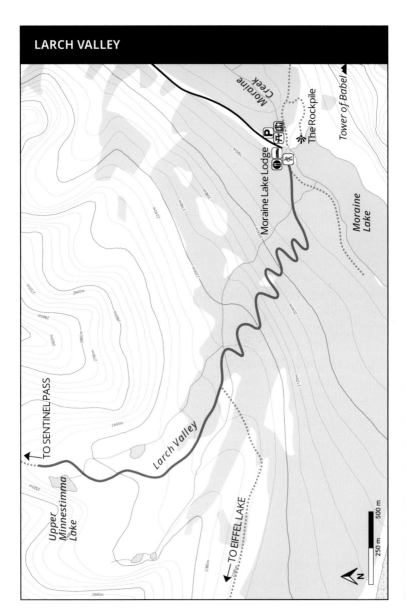

Mortaine Creek

Tower of Babel

The Rockpile

Moraine Lake Lodge

Moraine Lake

TO SENTINEL PASS

Larch Valley

TO EIFFEL LAKE

Upper Minnestimma Lake

250 m   500 m

N

LARCH VALLEY TRAIL OUTLINE

0.0 Trailhead (elevation 1,887 m/6,190 ft).
0.2 Junction. Larch Valley right.
1.1 Switchbacks begin. Steady climb.
2.4 Junction. Eiffel Lake left. Larch Valley right.
   —Climb into Larch Valley meadows.
4.5 Upper Minnestimma Lake (elevation 2,435 m/7,990 ft).

A stream flowing through Larch Valley.

Eiffel Lake

In 1894, before it was known as the Valley of the Ten Peaks, explorer Walter Wilcox and his companions named it Desolation Valley. In its most desolate heart is Eiffel Lake, reached by a high, contouring trail with views of the peaks that have made the valley famous.

NEED TO KNOW

LENGTH: 5.6 km (3.5 miles) one-way

ELEVATION GAIN: 410 m (1,360 ft)

WALKING TIME: 1.5 to 2 hours one-way

RATING: Moderate hike

SEASON: Late June to early October

INSIDER'S TIP

If you don't want to labour down over 200 metres (0.1 miles) of broken rock to reach Eiffel Lake, you can enjoy an overview of both lake and the Ten Peaks by continuing west along the trail to a sheltering grove of larch trees.

TRAILHEAD

Follow the Moraine Lake Road 12.5 kilometres (7.5 miles) to the parking area at Moraine Lake. Walk to the lakeshore and the trail sign below the lodge (N51°19.673' W116°10.899').

The Eiffel Lake trail follows the same course as the Larch Valley trail for the first 2.4 kilometres (1.5 miles), switchbacking upward through closed forest from the north end of Moraine Lake. Splitting near the lower edge of Larch Valley, the Eiffel Lake trail continues along the north side of the Valley of the Ten Peaks. It soon emerges onto open slopes where all of the ten summits are revealed across the valley as well as the brilliant blue waters of Moraine Lake far below.

As the trail continues through flower-filled meadows, the Wenkchemna Glacier is barely discernible in the valley below. Heavy rockfall from the cliffs above the glacier has completely covered most of its surface, shielding the ice from the sun's rays and accounting in part for the glacier's relatively small recession over the past century.

The trail reaches Eiffel Lake and the best viewpoint on a steep scree slope well above its shores. Reflecting upon one of his first visits to the lake, Walter Wilcox wrote: "It would be difficult to find another lake of small size in a wilder setting, the shores being of great angular stones, perfectly in harmony with the wild range of mountains beyond. Except in one place where a green and inviting slope comes down to the water, this rough ground is utterly unsuitable for vegetation and nearly devoid of trees."

Eiffel's rugged surroundings were created by a massive rockslide that broke away from Neptuak Mountain in the distant past and spread rock debris across the valley. Immediately above the lake to the north is Eiffel Peak (3,085 metres/10,120 feet), named for a rock pinnacle near its summit that resembles the famous Parisian tower.

OPTION

You can hike beyond Eiffel Lake for another four kilometres (2.5 miles) to **Wenkchemna Pass**, at 2,600 metres (8,530 feet) above sea level, and an outstanding viewpoint back across the Valley of the Ten Peaks.

The trail continues due west from the Eiffel Lake viewpoint across rolling alpine meadows, then climbs over moraine and along the rocky south ridge of Wenkchemna Peak before descending to the windswept gap between Wenkchemna Peak and Neptuak Mountain. (Sections of the trail may be obscured by snowfields before late July.)

Standing on the crest of the Great Divide, you overlook the entire length of the Valley of the Ten Peaks. On the west side of the divide is the rocky Eagle's Eyrie region of Yoho National Park and, further south, the forested headwaters of Tokumm Creek in Kootenay National Park.

OTHER NOTES

Travel on the Eiffel Lake trail may require a group of four people hiking in close proximity to one another if special restrictions concerning grizzly bears are in place.

The Moraine Lake area is very popular. Plan on arriving before 9am (and before 8am in July and August) to ensure a parking spot. When the parking lot is full, Moraine Lake Road is closed.

EIFFEL LAKE TRAIL OUTLINE

- **0.0**   Trailhead (elevation 1,887 m/6,190 ft).
- **0.2**   Junction. Eiffel Lake and Larch Valley right.
- **1.1**   Switchbacks begin. Steady climb.
- **2.4**   Junction. Larch Valley right. Eiffel Lake left.
   —Trail contours onto open slopes.
- **5.6**   Eiffel Lake viewpoint (elevation 2,300 m/7,550 ft).

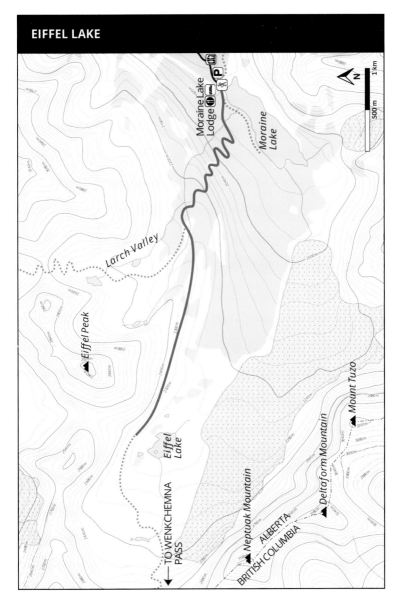

Moraine Lake Lodge

Moraine Lake

Larch Valley

Eiffel Peak

Eiffel Lake

TO WENKCHEMNA PASS

Neptuak Mountain

Deltaform Mountain

Mount Tuzo

ALBERTA

BRITISH COLUMBIA

N

1 km

500 m

Beyond the Larch Valley junction, open slopes allow sweeping valley views.

Consolation Lakes

The hike to Lower Consolation Lake is short and relatively flat, but the rugged scenery is as rewarding as that found on longer and more demanding trails in the region.

NEED TO KNOW

LENGTH: 2.9 km (1.8 miles) one-way

ELEVATION GAIN: 60 m (195 ft)

WALKING TIME: 45 minutes

RATING: Short hike

SEASON: Late June to early October

INSIDER'S TIP

Despite being a relatively flat, undemanding trail, it is often quite muddy. And if you want to visit Upper Consolation Lake, you might want to wear boots instead of running shoes.

TRAILHEAD

Follow Moraine Lake Road 12.5 km (7.5 miles) to the parking area at Moraine Lake. Walk down to the bridge over Moraine Creek, just below the lake outlet (N51°19.703' W116°10.872').

After crossing the Moraine Creek bridge just below the parking area, the trail passes over a substantial rockslide, which is the natural dam that created Moraine Lake. A short trail branches to the top of the Rockpile, where you are greeted by the classic view of Moraine Lake and the Valley of the Ten Peaks.

Beyond the rockslide, the trail enters a forest of spruce and fir and climbs gradually along the west side of Babel Creek. Just beyond the halfway point to the lake, the trail levels out along a meadow—a section that is often quite muddy.

A large rockslide blocks direct access to the north end of Lower Consolation Lake, but you still have a magnificent view of the lake and the glacier-capped summits of Bident and Quadra Mountains beyond. Mount Temple commands the view back down-valley to the north—at 3,544 metres (11,630 feet), the third highest mountain in Banff National Park and the highest in the Lake Louise-Moraine Lake vicinity.

OPTION

If you are visiting Consolation after the high-water period (June to mid-July) and want to spend a little more time in the area, you can visit **Upper Consolation Lake**. Cross Babel Creek below Lower Consolation Lake on rickety log booms and then follow a rough, muddy track along the lake's eastern shore. At the far end, climb over a ridge of rock debris separating the two lakes. (Good boots are required for this rocky scramble.)

OTHER NOTES

Travel on the Consolation Lakes trail may require a group of four people hiking in close proximity to one another if special restrictions concerning grizzly bears are in place.

CONSOLATION LAKES

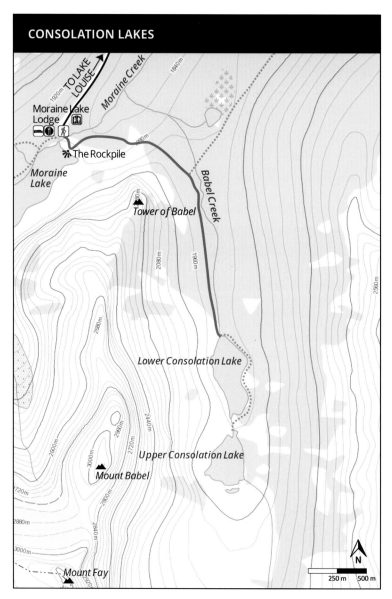

TO LAKE LOUISE →

1920 m

Moraine Creek

1840 m

Moraine Lake Lodge 🏨

🛏️🍴🚶

🏕️ The Rockpile

Moraine Lake

Babel Creek

Tower of Babel

2080 m

1960 m

2560 m

2680 m

Lower Consolation Lake

2440 m

2960 m

2720 m

Upper Consolation Lake

3000 m

Mount Babel

2800 m

2720 m

2880 m

3000 m

Mount Fay

N

250 m   500 m

CONSOLATION LAKES TRAIL OUTLINE

0.0 Trailhead (elevation 1,885 m/6,180 ft).
0.1 Junction. The Rockpile right. Consolation Lakes ahead.
      —Cross avalanche slope and a gradual climb through forest begins.
2.3 Open meadow.
2.9 Lower Consolation Lake (elevation 1,945 m/6,380 ft).

Looking across Lower Consolation Lake toward Mount Temple.

Lake Louise Gondola

During summer the main chairlift at Lake Louise Ski Resort whisks visitors up the face of Whitehorn Mountain in either open chairs or enclosed gondola cars to a slopeside viewpoint, interpretive centre, and the starting point for two hiking trails.

NEED TO KNOW

LENGTH: Up to 1.7 km (1.1 miles) one-way

ELEVATION GAIN: Up to 280 m (920 ft)

WALKING TIME: Up to 40 minutes one-way

RATING: Short hikes

SEASON: May to September daily 9am to 4pm
(until 5pm in July and August)

INSIDER'S TIP

When you purchase your gondola ticket, check for packages that may include breakfast or lunch for a small extra charge.

TRAILHEAD

To reach the gondola from the village, cross the Trans-Canada Highway and follow Whitehorn Road to the Lake Louise Ski Resort.

The view from where passengers disembark the gondola—at an altitude of more than two kilometres (1.2 miles) above sea level—is among the most spectacular in the Canadian Rockies. Views improve higher up, along the two trails described below.

Kicking Horse Viewpoint (0.9 kilometres/0.5 miles one-way), gaining around 150 metres (490 feet) of elevation as it traverses westward through forest and open ski runs to a lookout point where views extend across to the Great Divide. Allow around 40 minutes for the round trip.

The trail to **Ptarmigan Valley Viewpoint** is longer (1.7 km/1.1 mile each way) and gains more elevation (280 metres/920 feet), but hikers are rewarded with views north and east across the Ptarmigan Valley, as well as sweeping views across the Bow Valley to Lake Louise.

OTHER NOTES

The area between the bottom and the top of the gondola is prime grizzly bear habitat (you may see bears on the gondola ride) and is closed throughout summer, so you cannot access the upper slopes without riding the gondola, nor can you walk down from the upper terminal. It should also be noted that the two trails detailed above may be closed due to bear activity, so inquire at the base lodge before purchasing your gondola ticket.

From the Kicking Horse Viewpoint, Lake Louise is visible across the Bow Valley. Credit: Chris Moseley

Fireweed brightens the landscape along the trail to Ptarmigan Valley Viewpoint.

LAKE LOUISE GONDOLA

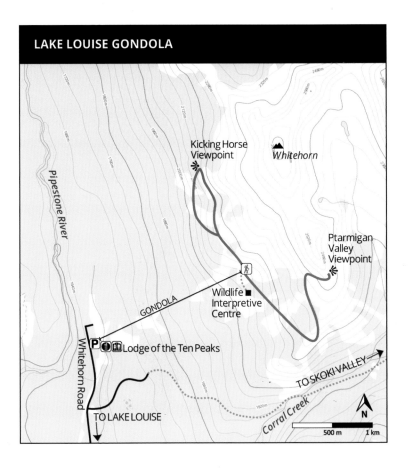

Kicking Horse Viewpoint

Whitehorn

Ptarmigan Valley Viewpoint

Pipestone River

GONDOLA

Wildlife Interpretive Centre

P Lodge of the Ten Peaks

Whitehorn Road

TO SKOKI VALLEY

TO LAKE LOUISE

Corral Creek

N

500 m   1 km

Mud Lake

For anyone in search of an escape from the bustling village of Lake Louise, Mud Lake is a pleasant if not overly spectacular destination.

NEED TO KNOW

LENGTH: 1.7 km (1.1 miles) one-way

ELEVATION GAIN: 50 m (150 ft)

WALKING TIME: 30 minutes one-way

RATING: Easy walk

SEASON: May to October

INSIDER'S TIP

Don't be put off by the name—Mud Lake is very clear. It reputedly got its name because wading in the shallows makes the water murky.

TRAILHEAD

Pipestone River Parking Area; follow the Trans-Canada Highway west 1.1 km (0.7 miles) from the Lake Louise exit to Slate Avenue (intersection also marked by "Pipestone" trail sign). Follow this paved road uphill to another intersection. Follow "Pipestone" trail sign to right and continue to the trailhead parking area (N51°26.014 W116°11.125').

This short and easy hike begins from the Pipestone River trailhead on the opposite side of the Trans-Canada Highway from the village of Lake Louise. As an alternative to driving, you can park near the end of Sheol Road (off the northwest end of Village Road) and cross the Trans-Canada Highway via the pedestrian bridge. Once across the highway, a well-worn trail leads up and across Slate Avenue. The trailhead is slightly downhill from this point.

Beyond the trailhead kiosk and access gate, you follow a rough service road that climbs gradually into dense pine forest. After 400 metres (0.2 miles), the Mud Lake and Pipestone River trails branch left from the road. In another 500 metres (0.3 miles), the Mud Lake trail forks uphill to the right from the broad Pipestone River track. From this final junction, it is under one kilometre (0.6 miles) to the lakeshore.

Mud Lake is just over 500 metres (0.3 miles) in length and encircled by a dense forest of lodgepole pine, but the lakeshore is open enough to allow views to Whitehorn and Lipalian Mountains to the north.

Climb through this gated entrance and you're on your way to Mud Lake.

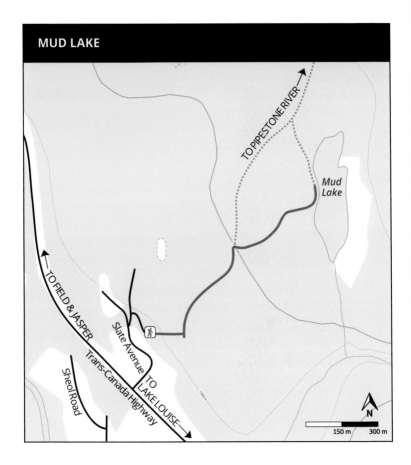

MUD LAKE TRAIL OUTLINE

- **0.0** Trailhead (elevation 1,555 m/5,100 ft).
- **0.4** Junction. Mud Lake left.
- **0.9** Junction. Pipestone River trail ahead. Mud Lake right.
- **1.7** Mud Lake (elevation 1,605 m/5,270 ft).

Unlike the name may suggest, Mud Lake is incredibly clear.

Credit: Leigh McAdam

Boulder Pass

Boulder Pass is the gateway to the Skoki Valley, an area of high valleys, passes and lakes that is one of the exceptional hiking areas in the Canadian Rockies.

NEED TO KNOW

LENGTH: 8.6 km (5.3 miles) one-way

ELEVATION GAIN: 655 m (2,150 ft)

WALKING TIME: 3 hours one-way

RATING: Day trip

SEASON: Late June to early October

INSIDER'S TIP

It's possible to continue into the Skoki Valley and return in a long day, but a better option is to book a backcountry campsite or reserve a bed at Skoki Lodge.

TRAILHEAD

From the Trans-Canada Highway interchange at Lake Louise, follow Whitehorn Road uphill toward the Lake Louise ski area. At 1.7 km (1.1 miles) turn right onto the gravel Fish Creek Road and follow it one km (0.6 miles) to the Fish Creek Parking Area (N51°26.411' W116°09.097').

The Boulder Pass trail begins at the Fish Creek Parking Area, just off the road linking the village of Lake Louise to Lake Louise Ski Resort. The first four kilometres (2.5 miles) of the trail along a gravel access road leading to the Temple Day Lodge (used in winter only by the ski area as a restaurant) will not bring joy to your heart, but it is the fastest way to the sublime landscape beyond. (Bikes are not permitted on this access road, though Skoki Lodge guests are transported up the road by van to begin their hike from the Temple Day Lodge.)

Once past the ski lifts at Temple, the road reverts to trail, which climbs steeply across a ski run and into a pleasant subalpine forest of spruce and fir with a scattering of alpine larch. The trail is wide and moderately graded, but since it is used for commercial horse trips and pack trains supplying Skoki Lodge, it is often quite muddy.

You soon reach the Corral Creek meadows, where there are views ahead to Boulder Pass and the rugged summits of Mount Richardson, Pika Peak and Ptarmigan Peak—the mountains that form the core of the Slate Range. Back to the southwest, 15 kilometres (9.3 miles) away, glacier-topped Mount Temple (3,544 metres/11,630 feet) dominates the skyline. The meadow is filled with a wide variety of colourful wildflowers in mid-summer, and slate-coloured dippers are often seen flying from rock to rock along nearby Corral Creek.

At km 7.1 (mile 4.4) you reach the junction for the 1.3-kilometre (0.8-mile) trail running north to Hidden Lake Campground and Hidden Lake. Halfway Hut sits on a low bluff just south of the junction. The log cabin received its name during the early days of skiing when it served as an overnight stop for skiers—halfway between the Lake Louise railway station and Skoki Lodge. Today it is a day-use-only shelter for hikers.

Beyond the Hidden Lake junction, the trail climbs through scattered forest to the summit of Boulder Pass and the west end of Ptarmigan

Lake. At an elevation of 2,345 metres (7,690 feet), this unique, lake-filled pass is at the upper limits of tree growth. There are open views down the lake to the distant peaks of Mount Douglas and Mount St. Bride, and the surrounding meadows and rockslides are well-populated with hoary marmots, pikas and white-tailed ptarmigan.

OPTION

The majority of hikers you will meet along this trail will be continuing over **Deception Pass** to **Skoki Valley**, where they use Skoki Lodge or the Merlin Meadows Campground as base camps for half-day to day long trips to nearby points of interest.

Strong day hikers can continue along the slopes above the north shore of Ptarmigan Lake then veer north and climb to Deception Pass, 2.4 kilometres (1.5 miles) and 130 metres (425 feet) of elevation gain from Boulder Pass. This rocky, alpine pass was named by Skoki ski pioneer Cyril Paris because he always thought its summit was closer than it really was when he was crossing it. From this lofty 2,475-metre-high (8,120-foot) vantage point, there is an all-encompassing view over the Ptarmigan Valley to Redoubt Mountain and through Boulder Pass to the distant mountains near Lake Louise. The pass is the best viewpoint on the trail and usually the farthest point reached by day hikers.

From Deception Pass the trail drops steadily northward into Skoki Valley. Views to the west include Ptarmigan Peak and the turquoise Skoki Lakes—Myosotis and Zigadenus (genus names for the forget-me-not and camas lily). After descending over rocky slopes and alpine meadows, the trail passes through scattered alpine larch and re-enters the forest, reaching **Skoki Lodge** 14.4 kilometres (nine miles) from the Fish Creek trailhead. The rustic lodge with outlying cabins provides accommodation and meals for guests throughout the summer and winter months. For information visit www.skokilodge.com.

The approach to Deception Pass
Credit: Leigh McAdam

Historic Skoki Lodge is the destination of many hikers travelling over Boulder Pass. Credit: Chris Moseley

BOULDER PASS TRAIL OUTLINE

0.0 Trailhead (elevation 1,690 m/5,540 ft).
　　　—Follow Temple access road.
3.9 Temple Day Lodge.
　　　—Trail climbs across ski slope for 200 metres (0.1 miles) and
　　　　enters forest.
6.3 Corral Creek meadows.
7.1 Junction. Hidden Lake left. Halfway Hut right. Boulder Pass ahead.
　　　—Steady uphill.
8.6 Boulder Pass (elevation 2,345 m/7,690 ft).

The view into Skoki Valley from Deception Pass. Credit: Leigh McAdam

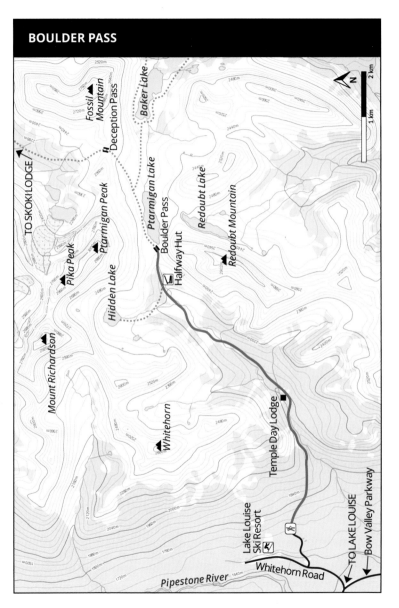

BOULDER PASS

N

1 km
2 km

Fossil Mountain

Deception Pass

Baker Lake

TO SKOKI LODGE

Ptarmigan Peak

Pika Peak

Ptarmigan Lake

Boulder Pass

Halfway Hut

Redoubt Lake

Redoubt Mountain

Hidden Lake

Mount Richardson

Whitehorn

Temple Day Lodge

Lake Louise Ski Resort

Whitehorn Road

Pipestone River

TO LAKE LOUISE

Bow Valley Parkway

Index